SILLY JOKES FOR 6 YEAR OLDS

Why did the boy throw the butter into the sky?

He wanted to see a butter-fly!

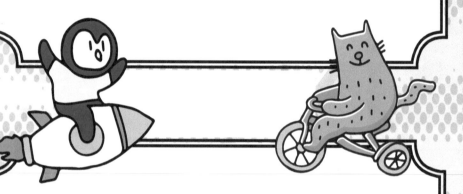

Why do penguins always carry fish in their beaks?

Because penguins don't have pockets!

Why don't cat's love pink the most?

Because their favorite color is purrrr-ple!

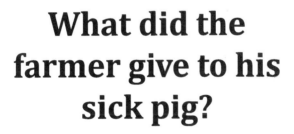

What did the farmer give to his sick pig?

Some oink-ment!

What was the baby doing in Egypt?

It couldn't find its mummy!

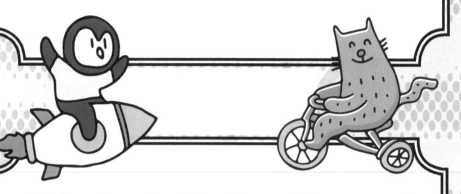

Why isn't Cinderella good at football?

Because she runs away from the ball!

What do you call a T-Rex that's fast asleep?

A dino-snore!

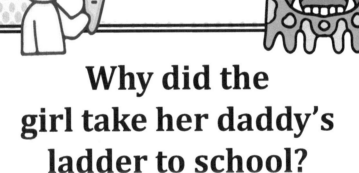

Why did the girl take her daddy's ladder to school?

She couldn't wait to go to high school!

Why didn't the postman know the alphabet?

Because he lost all his letters!

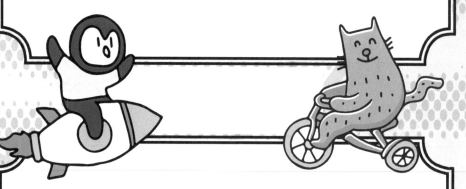

What happens when you cross a rabbit with a frog?

You get a bunny ribbit

What did the wind say to the tree?

I'll leaf you alone now!

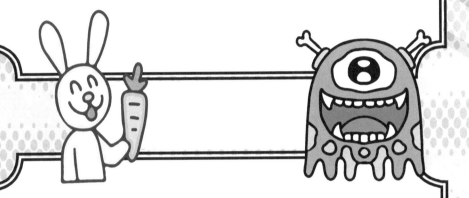

Why did the melon get into the bathtub?

He wanted to become a watermelon!

Knock, knock.
Who's there?
Tank.
Tank who?
Thank me?! But I didn't do anything!

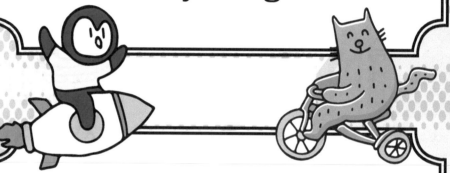

What do you call a chewy bear that has no teeth?

A gummy bear!

Why should you never give your balloon to Elsa from Frozen?

She'll just "let it go, let it go!"

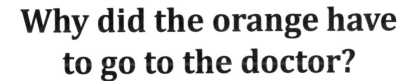

Why did the orange have to go to the doctor?

It wasn't peeling very well!

What do you call a famous fish actor?

A starfish!

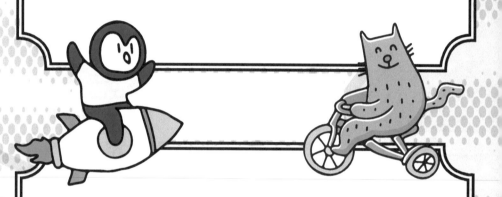

Which superhero is the best baseball player?

Batman!

Do you know what the pumpkin said to the pie?

Nothing! Pumpkins can't talk, silly!

Which sort of market do dogs never go to?

The flea market!

What begins with t, ends with t, and has t inside of it?

A teapot!

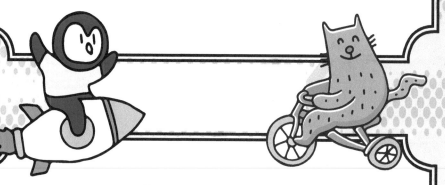

Guess what the right eye said to the left eye?

Between you and me, something smells!

What does a vet do when they get a sick bird?

They give it some tweet-ment!

Knock, knock.
Who's there?
The interrupting sheep

**(The interrupt..)
BAAH!**

What goes black, white, bump, black, white, bump?

A panda falling downstairs!

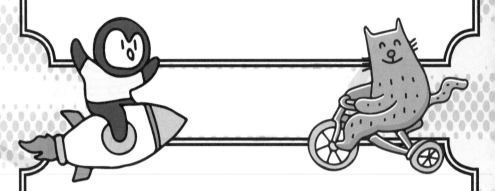

Why should an egg never tell jokes?

Because it might crack itself up!

Which is the smartest insect?

A spelling bee!

What do you call cows that can play the piano?

Moosicians!

What's the first thing elves learn when they go to school?

The letters of the elf-abet!

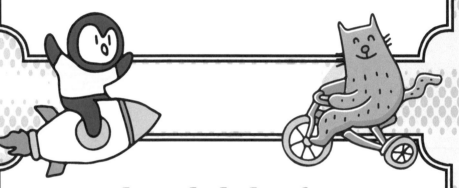

What did the first snowman say to the second snowman?

I keep smelling carrots!

Why did the cats put on walking boots?

They wanted to climb the meow-tain!

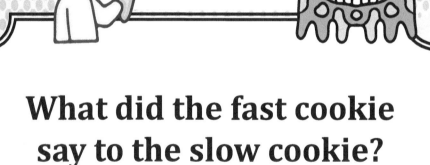

What did the fast cookie say to the slow cookie?

Crumb on!

Why was the spider so excited to get married?

Because she wanted to see her webbing dress!

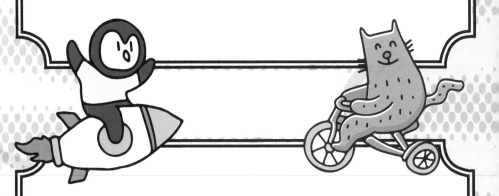

Which fairy never takes a shower?

Stinkerbell.

What is a toad's favorite fizzy drink?

Croak-a-Cola!

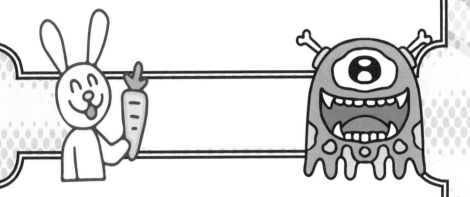

What is an Italian ghost's favorite food?

Spook-etti!

Knock, knock.
Who's there?
Woo.
Woo who?
Woah! What are you so excited about?!

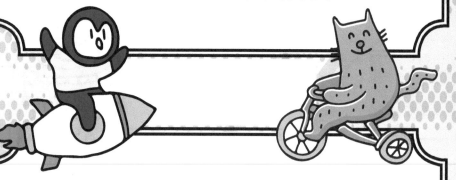

Why did the baker put her cake in the freezer?

She thought it needed more icing!

What is completely orange and sounds like parrot?

A carrot!

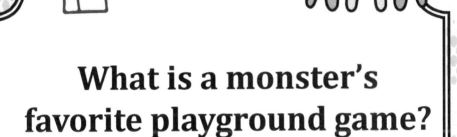

What is a monster's favorite playground game?

Swallow the leader!

Which planet is the best at singing?

Nep-tune!

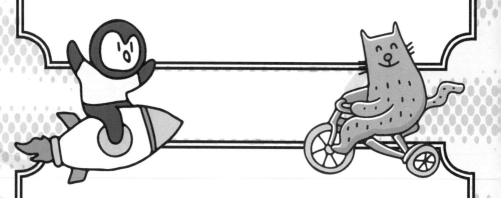

What did one finger say to the other finger?

I'm in glove with you!

What happens when you shake up a cow?

You get milkshake!

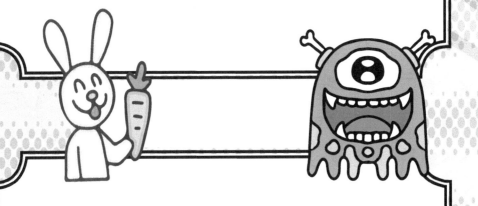

What's green and smells like red paint?

Green paint!

What made the jelly wobble?

*The jelly
saw a milk shake!*

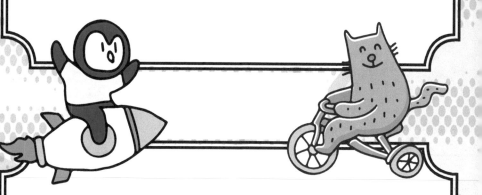

What happened when seven was hungry?

Seven eight nine!

What was the witch's favorite part of English at school?

Spelling!

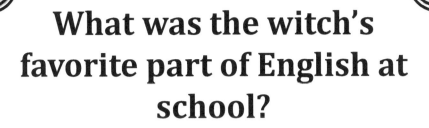

Where do cats go to learn about history?

To the mewseum!

What is a dinosaur with no eyes called?

A do-you-think-it-saurus!

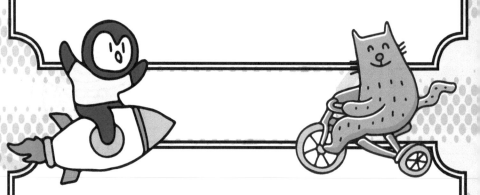

What kind of dog likes washing its hair?

A sham-poodle!

What does a cat say after it hurts its paw?

Meow-ch!

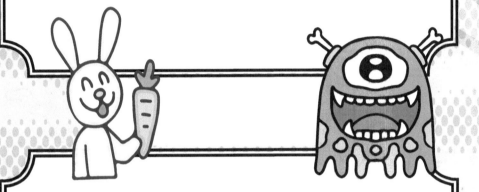

Where is a pencil's favorite place to go on vacation?

Pencil-vania!

What is very sticky and brown?

A stick!

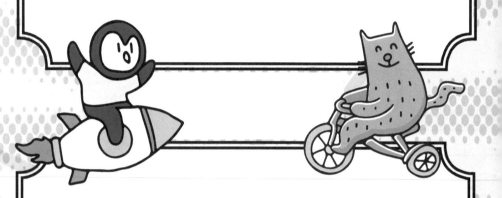

What kind of cat does everything its owner does?

A copycat!

What flies in the sky and wobbles?

A jelly-copter!

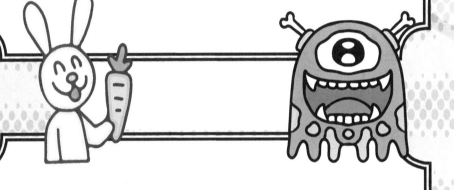

What type of shoes does a burglar wear?

Sneakers!

What type of key can open bananas?

A mon-key!

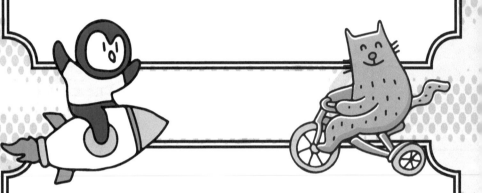

Why do giraffes have long necks?

They have very smelly feet!

How does an ocean say hello to the sea?

It waves!

Knock knock.
Who's there?
Cabbage.
Cabbage who?
Cabbage doesn't have a last name, silly!

How does a basketball arena stay nice and cool during a game?

Because it has lots of fans!

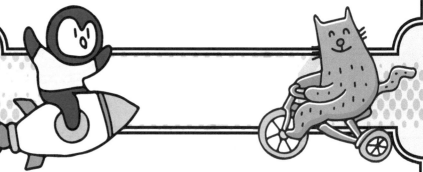

Knock knock.
Who's there?
Canoe.
Canoe who?
Canoe just come outside and play already?!

What is a sneezing train called?

Atchoo-choo train!

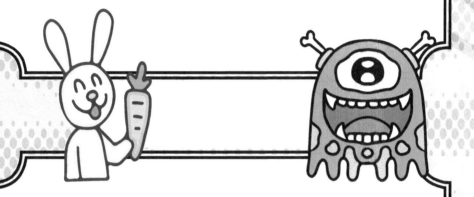

Where does a fish keep all of its money?

In a river bank!

Knock knock.
Who's there?
Ach.
Ach who?
Oh my! Bless you!

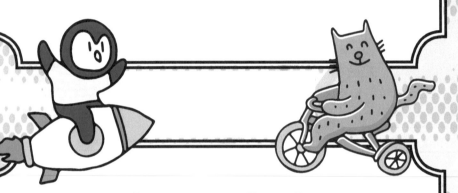

What made the rabbit feel so happy?

He found out some bunny loved him!

Which is the worst vegetable for a sailor?

A leek!

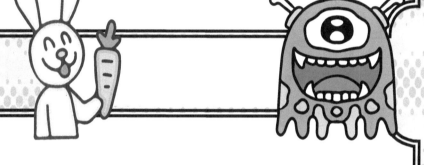

What type of witch would you find down at the beach?

A sand-witch!

What is a sea monster's favorite meal?

Fish and ships!

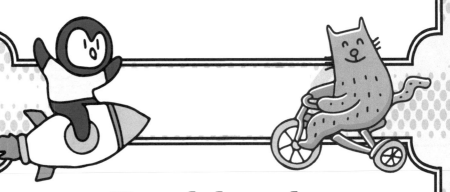

Knock knock.
Who's there?
Icy.
Icy who?
I see you looking at me!

What is a deer that has no eyes?

No eye-deer!

Why is the giant so clever?

Because he uses lots of big words!

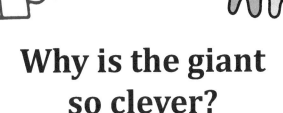

What is slippery and a foot long?

Your slipper!

What do you say to a horse that lives next door to you?

Hello neigh-bor!

Where should you take a horse when it's sick?

To the horse-pital!

Knock. knock
Who's there?
Cow.
Cow who?
Cows don't go 'who', they go mooo!

What does a cat wear to bed?

Paw-jamas!

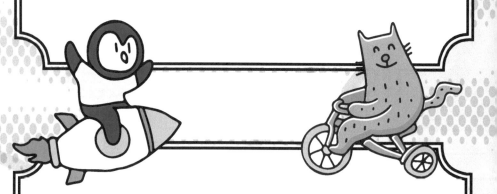

Where does Tarzan get all his clothes from?

A jungle sale!

What did the mom volcano say to the baby volcano?

I lava you very much!

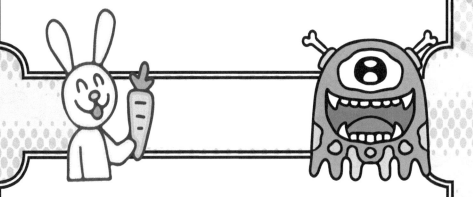

What did the scarf tell the hat?

I'll wait here, you go a-head!

What happens if you put a skunk inside a helicopter?

You get a smelly-copter!

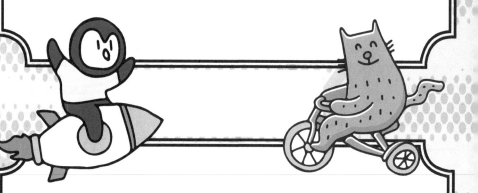

What is a dog's favorite pizza?

Pupperoni pizza!

Knock knock.
Who's there?
Radio.
Radio who?
**Ready or not,
here I come!**

**What kind of shoes can
you make from bananas?**

Yellow slippers!

Knock knock.
Who's there?
Ice cream soda.
Ice cream soda who?
I scream so that you can hear me clearly!

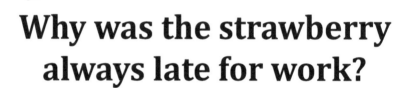

Why was the strawberry always late for work?

It always gets into a traffic jam!

What do you get if a seagull flies over a bay?

A bay-gull!

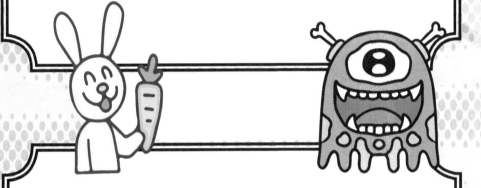

What do you call someone else's cheese?

Nacho cheese!

Why did the skeleton cross the road?

So it could get to the body shop!

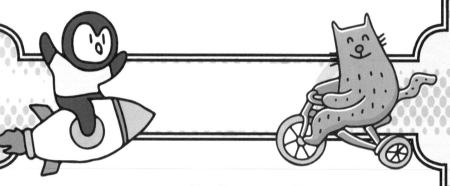

Knock knock.
Who's there?
Kanga.
Kanga who?
It's kanga-roo, actually!

What is the worst kind of music for balloons?

Pop music!

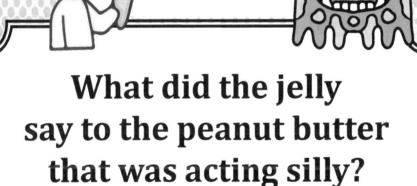

What did the jelly say to the peanut butter that was acting silly?

You're just nuts!

Why do math books look sad all the time?

Because they have too many problems!"

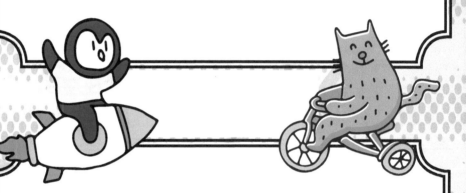

What does a polar bear love to eat?

Icebergers!

How can you make an octopus laugh?

By giving it ten-tickles!

How do you know if you have an elephant underneath your bed?

Your nose will touch the ceiling!

Do you know why Pirates are called Pirates?

They just Arrrrr!

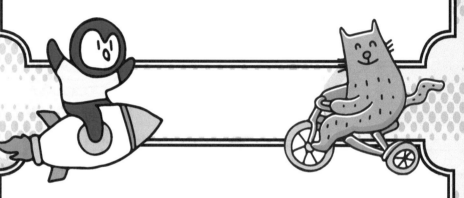

Why is cold so bad at tag?

Because anyone can catch a cold!

What does the Hulk love to drink?

Green tea!

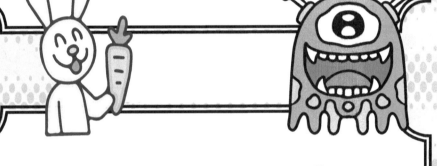

What is a cow who chews up your lawn called?

A lawn-mooer!

What can fall down in winter and never get hurt?

Snow!

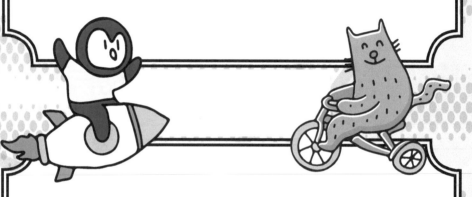

What does the man at the paint shop say to answer the phone?

Yellow!

What is a fish that has no eyes called?

A fsh!

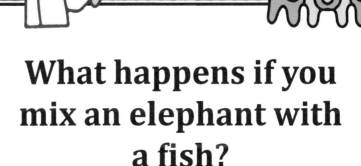

What happens if you mix an elephant with a fish?

Huge swimming trunks!

What do you call a donkey that only has three legs?

A wonkey!

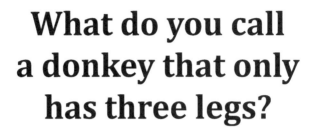

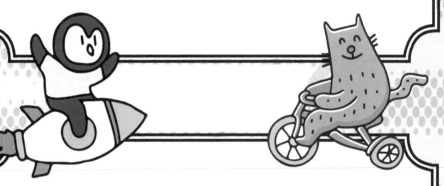

Knock knock.
Who's there?
I eep.
I eep who?
Eww! That's gross!

What does everyone always get on their birthday?

A year older!

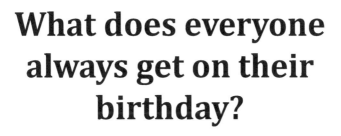

Why does a hummingbird always hum?

Because it doesn't know the words!

Knock knock.
Who's there?
Pile up.
Pile up who?
Eww! Where?!

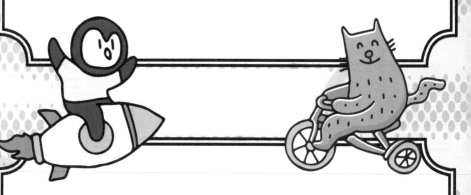

**What would a slice
of toast wear to sleep in?**

Pa-JAM-as!

What do you get when a pear falls over?

Pear drops!

How do you start off a teddy bear's race?

Ready! Teddy! Go!

Why must birds fly south every winter?

Because it's too far for them to walk!

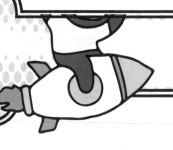

Why is bees hair always sticky?

They always use honey-combs!

What letter of the alphabet is really wet?

The C!

Which animal loves playing baseball?

A bat!

What kind of chip can fly?

A rocket chip!

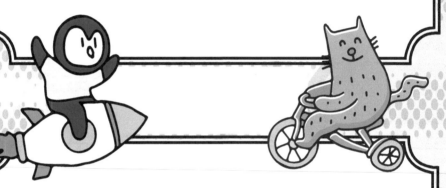

What happens when you cross a kangaroo and a sheep?

You get a woolly jumper!

What is yellow and looks like small pineapple?

A lemon with a haircut!

What is a scarecrow's favorite kind of cake?

Straw-berry cake!

What did the cop say to the robber's belly?

Stop you're under a vest!

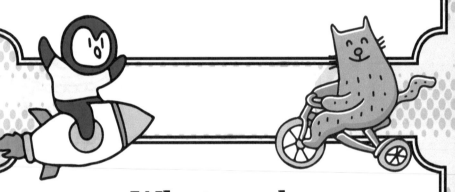

What made Mickey Mouse go into outer space?

He needed to find Pluto!

What does a detective look for at Christmas time?

Santa Clues!

What do pigs live in at the North Pole?

Pig-loos!

What is a ghost's favorite dessert?

I scream!

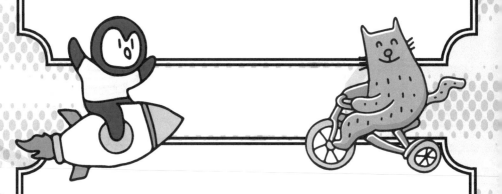

Which monster is always the best dancer at parties?

The boogie-man!

Where does a polar bear go to get their money?

A snow bank!

How does a dinosaur cut wood?

With a dino-saw!

What should you say to a gorilla with bananas in its ears?

It doesn't matter, it can't hear you!

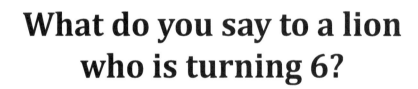

What do you say to a lion who is turning 6?

It's roar birthday!

What does a little corn need after a hug from mama corn?

A hug from pop corn!

Why was the broom so late for class?

It overswept!

What does a witch always spread on a bagel?

Lots of scream cheese!

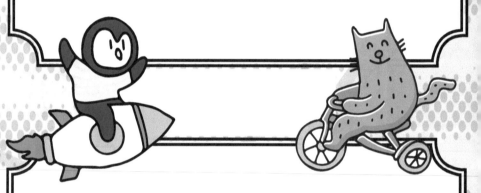

What is a cat's favorite dessert?

Mice cream!

What is a peanut in a space rocket called?

An astro-nut!

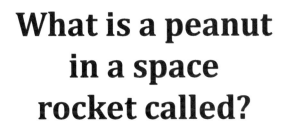

What is the richest fish in the sea?

A goldfish!

Why should you never play checkers in the jungle?

There are way too many cheetahs!

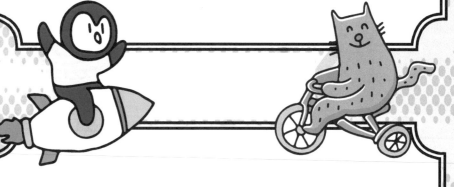

What did the mama tomato say to her baby tomato?

Try to ketchup!

What should you say to a rabbit on it's birthday?

Hoppy Birthday!

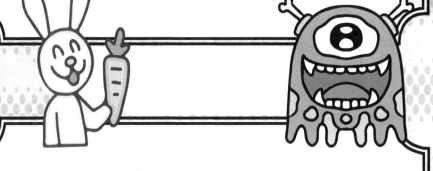

What did the photographer say to the pizza?

Smile and say cheese!

How does a unicorn ride to the park?

On its uni-cycle!

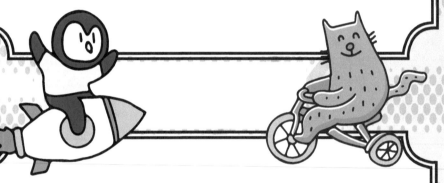

Why can't the skeleton go to the dance?

It has no-body to go with!

What happens if you pour hot chocolate down a rabbit hole at easter?

You get hot cross bunnies!

Do you know many apples grow on apple trees?

They all do!

Made in United States
Troutdale, OR
12/02/2024

25646138R00046